About This Book

Title: *Pigs*

Step: 1

I0821175

Word Count: 99

Skills in Focus: All short vowels

Tricky Words: are, this, nose, be, you, farm, sees, ground, corn, with

Ideas for Using This Book

Before Reading:

- **Comprehension:** Look at the title and cover image together. Ask readers what they know about pigs. What new things do they think they might learn in this book?
- **Accuracy:** Practice saying the tricky words listed on page 1.
- **Phonemic Awareness:** Tell readers you will practice taking apart and putting together the sounds in the word *pig*. Ask readers to tap each finger to their thumb to count the sounds they hear. Ask: How many sounds are in the word *pig*? What is the first sound? Middle sound? End sound? Change the /p/ to /b/. What word is it? Repeat with the word *dig*. Change the /d/ to /w/. Ask students to name other -*ig* words they know.

During Reading:

- Have readers point under each word as they read it.
- **Decoding:** If readers are stuck on a word, help them say each sound and blend the sounds together smoothly. Be sure to point out any short vowel sounds as they appear.
- **Comprehension:** Invite students to talk about what new things they are learning about pigs while reading. What are they learning that they didn't know before?

After Reading:

Discuss the book. Some ideas for questions:

- Do you like pigs? Why or why not?
- How are pigs similar to other animals you have learned about? How are they different?

Pigs

Text by Haley Williams

Reading Consultant
Deborah MacPhee, PhD
Professor, School of Teaching and Learning
Illinois State University

PICTURE WINDOW BOOKS
a capstone imprint

Kids can pet pigs.

Pigs can get big.
Hogs are big pigs.

This pig is not big.

Pigs are put in pens.

Pigs nap in pens.

The pigs get fed corn.

Pigs can get fat.

A pig digs with its nose.

It digs in the ground.

Pigs can get hot.

This pig sits in the mud.
Now it is not hot!

Pigs run in the mud.
The mud is on the pigs!

A pig is on a farm.
It sees a hen.

It sees a dog.

Pigs can be pets.

Pet pigs are fun!

Will you pet a pig?

More Ideas:

Phonemic Awareness Activity

Practicing Short Vowels:

Say a short vowel story word for readers to practice breaking apart the sounds. Tell readers to make a movement such as hopping in place or tapping a finger on the table as they break apart the word, saying each sound. Begin with *pig*. They will make one movement for /p/, again for /i/, and once more for /g/. What sound was first? Middle sound? Ending sound?

Suggested words:

- hog
- pet
- mud
- pen
- dig

Extended Learning Activity

Let's Draw!

This book is about pigs. Ask readers to draw a picture of a pig on a piece of paper. Then ask readers to share a sentence or two about pigs. Have students use words with short vowel sounds in their sentences.

Published by Picture Window Books, an imprint of Capstone
1710 Roe Crest Drive, North Mankato, Minnesota 56003
capstonepub.com

Copyright © 2026 by Capstone.
All rights reserved. No part of this publication may be reproduced in whole or in part, or stored in a retrieval system, or transmitted in any form or by any means, electronic, mechanical, photocopying, recording, or otherwise, without written permission of the publisher.

Library of Congress Cataloging-in-Publication Data is available on the Library of Congress website.

ISBN: 9798875277146 (hardback)
ISBN: 9798875277108 (paperback)
ISBN: 9798875277085 (eBook PDF)

Image Credits: Getty: ChristiLaLiberte, 16-17, gumboot, 14-15, Luis Sotillo, 8-9, rtyree1, front cover, schankz, 11, shaunl, 12, 24, SolStock, 10; Shutterstock: Anicka.M, 18, Chachamp, 4-5, Dmitry Kalinovsky, 2-3, Eric Isselee, 1, 7, Lois GoBe, 13, MintImages, 21, New Africa, 20, Rita_ Kochmarjova, 19, sergio victor vega, 6, back cover, The Len, 22-23

Printed and bound in China. PO 6460